AMERICA'S INDUSTRIAL SOCIETY IN THE 19TH CENTURY ™

Oil, Steel, and Railroads

America's Big Businesses in the Late 1800s

Jesse Jarnow

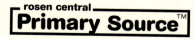
rosen central
Primary Source ™

The Rosen Publishing Group, Inc., New York

Published in 2004 by The Rosen Publishing Group, Inc.
29 East 21st Street, New York, NY 10010

First Edition

Library of Congress Cataloging-in-Publication Data

Jarnow, Jesse.
Oil, steel, and railroads: America's big businesses in the late 1800s/by Jesse Jarnow.
    v. cm.—(America's industrial society in the 19th century)
Includes bibliographical references and index.
Contents: From sea to shining sea—Andrew Carnegie and the steel revolution—Black gold.
ISBN 0-8239-4023-3 (library binding)
ISBN 0-8239-4276-7 (paperback)
6-pack ISBN 0-8239-4288-0
1. Big business—United States—History—19th century—Juvenile literature. 2. Industrial concentration—United States—History—19th century—Juvenile literature. 3. Industries—United States—History—19th century—Juvenile literature. [1. Industrial revolution. 2. Railroads—History —19th century. 3. Steel industry and trade—History—19th century. 4. Petroleum industry and trade—History—19th century.]
I. Title. II. Series.
HD2356.U5 J37 2003
338.6'44'097309034—dc21

                                                                    2002153979

Manufactured in the United States of America

On the cover: large image: repairing railroad line, Virginia, Confederate States of America, 1864. First row (from left to right): steamship docked at a landing; Tammany Hall on election night, 1859; map showing U.S. railroad routes in 1883; detail of bank note, 1822, Bank of the Commonwealth of Kentucky; People's Party (Populist) Convention at Columbus, Nebraska, 1890; Republican ticket, 1865. Second row (from left to right): William McKinley gives a campaign speech in 1896; parade banner of the Veterans of the Haymarket Riot; Alexander Graham Bell's sketch of the telephone, c. 1876; public declaration of the government's ability to crush monopolies; city planners' illustration of Stockton, California; railroad construction camp, Nebraska, 1889.

Photo credits: cover, pp. 6, 11, 13, 15, 18 © Library of Congress; p. 5 © Hulton/Archive/Getty Images; p. 9 © Library of Congress, Geography and Map Division; p. 12 Courtesy of the Bruce Gurner Collection, Water Valley Casey Jones Railroad Museum, J. E. France; p. 16 © Erich Hutton; p. 20 © Bettmann/Corbis; p. 22 © Library of Congress, Prints and Photographs Division; p. 25 © Underwood and Underwood/Corbis.

Designer: Tahara Hasan; **Editor:** Jill Jarnow

Contents

1
From Sea to Shining Sea

The Industrial Revolution began in England in the early 1700s. Machines replaced hand tools. People could make cloth and do other jobs more quickly than ever before. At first, water powered the machines. Then, in 1763, James Watt invented a steam engine. The world would never be the same.

Samuel Homfray lived in Wales. In 1803, Homfray and friends watched a horse pull a wagon along a tram rail. Homfray bet the others that a steam engine could do the same job as the horse.

Homfray went to Richard Trevithick. This man knew how to build small steam engines. Trevithick built a very powerful steam engine for Homfray. In 1804, Homfray's engine pulled the first passenger train. The engine and cars had special metal wheels that ran on iron rails. The train carried seventy people. It also pulled ten tons of iron

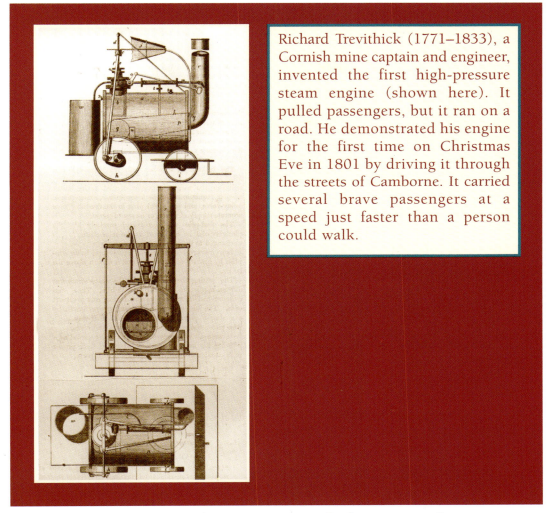

Richard Trevithick (1771–1833), a Cornish mine captain and engineer, invented the first high-pressure steam engine (shown here). It pulled passengers, but it ran on a road. He demonstrated his engine for the first time on Christmas Eve in 1801 by driving it through the streets of Camborne. It carried several brave passengers at a speed just faster than a person could walk.

and five wagons. The train traveled nine miles in two hours. Homfray won the bet.

England was already crowded with cities and towns, but the United States was growing. Trains would be more useful there.

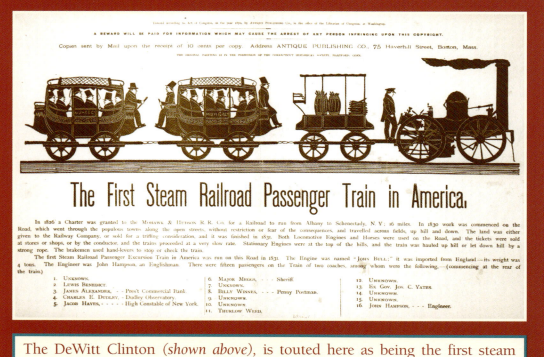

The First Steam Railroad Passenger Train in America.

In 1826 a Charter was granted to the MOHAWK & HUDSON R. R. Co. for a Railroad to run from Albany to Schenectady, N. Y.; 16 miles. In 1830 work was commenced on the Road, which went through the populous towns along the open streets, without restriction or fear of the consequences, and travelled across fields, up hill and down. The land was either given to the Railway Company, or sold for a trifling consideration, and it was finished in 1831. Both Locomotive Engines and Horses were used on the Road, and the tickets were sold at stores or shops, or by the conductor, and the trains proceeded at a very slow rate. Stationary Engines were at the top of the hills, and the train was hauled up hill or let down hill by a strong rope. The brakemen used hand-levers to stop or check the train.

The first Steam Railroad Passenger Excursion Train in America was run on this Road in 1831. The Engine was named "JOHN BULL;" it was imported from England—its weight was 4 tons. The Engineer was John Hampson, an Englishman. There were fifteen passengers on the Train of two coaches, among whom were the following,—(commencing at the rear of the train.)

1. UNKNOWN.	6. MAJOR MEGGS, - - - Sheriff.	12. UNKNOWN.
2. LEWIS BENEDICT.	7. UNKNOWN.	13. EX GOV. JOS. C. YATES.
3. JAMES ALEXANDER, - - Pres't Commercial Bank.	8. BILLY WINNES, - - - Penny Postman.	14. UNKNOWN.
4. CHARLES E. DUDLEY, - Dudley Observatory.	9. UNKNOWN.	15. UNKNOWN.
5. JACOB HAYES, - - - - - High Constable of New York.	10. UNKNOWN.	16. JOHN HAMPSON, - - - Engineer.
	11. THURLOW WEED.	

The DeWitt Clinton *(shown above)*, is touted here as being the first steam engine to pull a passenger train in America. This image records the passengers on that day, August 9, 1831, when it traveled between Albany and Schenectady, New York. Some historians believe that the first steam engine to pull passengers in America was the Best Friend, which ran on the Charleston Railroad in South Carolina. Others say it was a British-made engine, the John Bull.

In the 1820s, a group of American businessmen went to England to learn about railroads. At the time, goods and people in the United States were traveling by canal boats and wagons. The businessmen wanted to build railroads in America. They could earn a lot of money.

Americans who ran stagecoaches, canals, taverns, and toll roads were unhappy because they knew railroads would put them out of business. They tried to prevent railroads from being built. But they couldn't.

Men began to lay train tracks in the United States in the 1830s. Gold was discovered in California in 1848.

Trouble Ahead

The years after the Civil War were called the Golden Age of the Railroad. The owners of the railroads, steel mills, and oil companies got very rich. Men like John D. Rockefeller and Andrew Carnegie made fortunes on the new technologies. Their companies did a lot of good: They helped America grow and prosper. Railroads helped people live in greater comfort. People could travel and get news more quickly. People could live in more places, too.

But the railroads also did a lot of harm. They displaced hundreds of thousands of Native Americans. Railroad companies underpaid their workers. Smoke and soot from the railroad engines damaged the environment.

The lure of wealth made people want to travel to the West. A train could get them there quickly. But in 1854, tracks only went as far west as the Mississippi River.

By 1860, about 30,000 miles of rails had been laid. The Civil War began in 1861. Most railroad tracks were in the North. Soldiers battled to control them. The Northern army used trains to carry supplies to battlefronts. This helped them win the war.

In 1862, President Abraham Lincoln approved the building of more railroad tracks. They would run across the country. Tracks would be laid across the frontier. People would be able to travel by train to California!

A lot of companies got into the act. Newspapers reported on the building of the railroad. People liked to read about famous magnates, including Jay Gould, Cornelius Vanderbilt, and Jim Fisk.

Readers followed the railroad companies like sports teams. There were races to see who could lay down the most tracks and who would reach a certain city the fastest.

Many railroad workers were immigrants from Asia and Ireland. They worked very long hours. They toiled in terrible heat and freezing cold. They suffered so their bosses could meet deadlines.

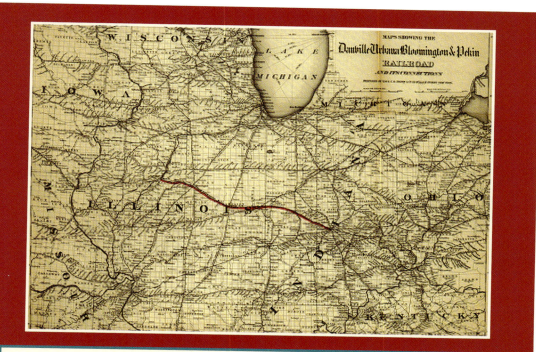

This map of midwestern states, created in 1869, depicts the Danville, Urbana, Bloomington, and Pekin Railroad lines. In addition to showing the connecting rails lines, the map notes the locations of towns, cities, and counties. Emphasizing its main rail line, the map gives mileage between the stations.

One set of tracks was built from California toward the East. Another set of tracks was laid from Nebraska toward the West. The tracks cut right through lands that belonged to Native Americans. The train companies asked the government to pass special bills for them. The

🛡 The First Unions

The business of trains has had many lasting effects. Train workers formed the country's first labor unions. The unions fought for better working conditions, job safety, and better pay. The improvements they won helped all workers in the United States.

bills allowed them to take land from the Native Americans. The railroad companies felt no guilt. They were run by greedy men.

The two railroad lines met in Utah in 1869. There was a huge celebration. The lines were joined by a golden spike. Trains could now cross America. They formed the first transcontinental railroad. People could travel by train from the Atlantic Ocean to the Pacific Ocean.

Business magnates owned their own fancy train cars. By 1869, rich people could ride across the country in trains

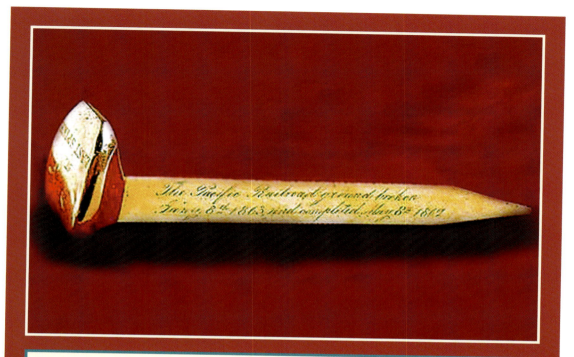

The golden spike (*above*) that reportedly was used to attach the final rails of the Transcontinental Railroad now resides in the Stanford University Museum of Art in California. After the ceremony on May 10, 1869, the spike, which was too soft to hold a rail in place, was given to Leland Stanford, president of the Central Pacific Railroad, by engraver David Hewes.

with Silver Palace cars, which were deluxe sleeping and dining cars.

But everyone else, rich or poor, rode together. This helped bring many people together for the first time. Still,

there was a lot of prejudice in America. At the stations, men and women used separate waiting rooms. Black people and white people were not allowed to wait together.

The trains stopped at Harvey Houses for food. Harvey House was one of the first chain restaurants. Passengers watched buffalo graze in the grass. And every now and then, there would be a train robbery.

Train Songs

The men who built the railroad hammered in rhythm. To pass the time, they sang folk songs, including "Drill Ye Tarriers." They sang about fallen heroes Casey Jones and John Henry.

People could tell who was driving the trains by the different whistles used by the engineers. They could tell the time based on when they heard the whistles in the distance.

Engineer Casey Jones (1863–1900) became famous for his daring deeds when Wallace Saunders, an African American railroad worker, wrote a song about his tragic death.

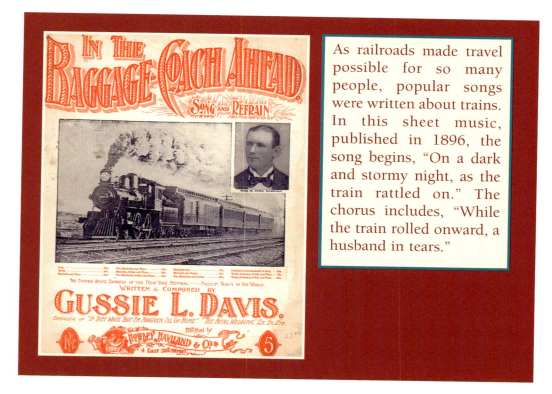

As railroads made travel possible for so many people, popular songs were written about trains. In this sheet music, published in 1896, the song begins, "On a dark and stormy night, as the train rattled on." The chorus includes, "While the train rolled onward, a husband in tears."

Before there were trains, most people in the United States lived on the East Coast. The railroads helped the country grow. Now, people could live in the middle and western parts of the United States. They could get supplies and news faster than ever before. Trains carried people westward into the future.

2

Andrew Carnegie and the Steel Revolution

Andrew Carnegie was born in Scotland. In 1848, his family sailed for America. They wanted a better life. Andrew was 12 years old.

The immigrant family arrived in New York. They traveled by canal until they reached Pittsburgh, Pennsylvania. That's where they settled.

Andrew earned money. He worked with new machines in a mill. He delivered messages. He operated the telegraph. He worked for a railroad. At night, he went to school. And he read a lot of books.

Carnegie's jobs became more important. He began to earn more money. He invested his money in companies.

He invested in the Keystone Bridge Company. In 1865, he became its manager. This company built iron bridges for railroads.

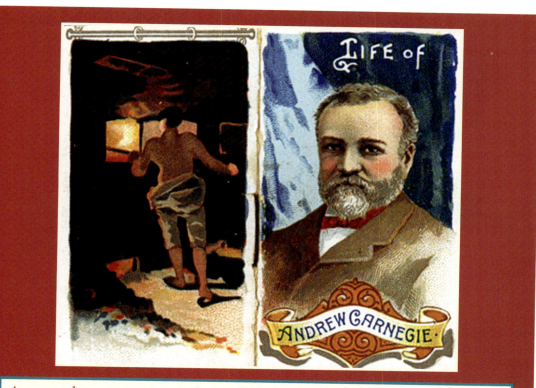

As poor boys grew up to be millionaires or celebrities in the United States, they became the subjects of excitement and curiosity for many people who wished they could be so successful. This portrait of Andrew Carnegie appeared in a booklet produced to advertise Duke Cigarettes. Other people portrayed in the series were Thomas Edison and Cornelius Vanderbilt.

Andrew Carnegie went to Britain every summer. There he met the inventor Henry Bessemer. Bessemer had invented a method to make steel. It was called the Bessemer process.

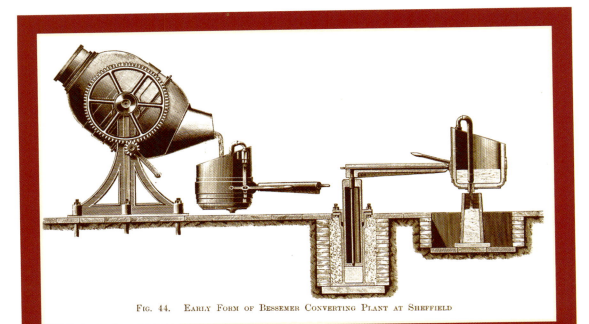

FIG. 44.   EARLY FORM OF BESSEMER CONVERTING PLANT AT SHEFFIELD

From the autobiography of Sir Henry Bessemer (1813–1898), published in 1905, this page shows an early version of the equipment he developed for his plant in Sheffield, England, where he invented the way to convert metal into steel. Bessemer, who had been fascinated with machinery and metal since childhood, spent his life as an inventor.

Steel was much stronger than iron. Carnegie saw that steel was the future. He could use this new material to make better railroad tracks. He could build machines, bridges, and buildings with steel.

Around 1873, Carnegie started a steel company. By 1889, the Carnegie Steel Company was a big success.

Westward Ho!

After the Civil War, the government created a federal land grant program. It helped people move to the West. It also helped pay for more railroads.

However, the train was a very dangerous way to travel. Bridges, tracks, and roadbeds were weak. There were many bad accidents. But Carnegie's steel tracks were a lot stronger and safer than iron rails.

Carnegie's company worked in many parts of the steel industry. It bought land that had huge iron ore deposits. Iron ore is a raw material that is turned into steel.

The Carnegie Steel Company did research, too. It developed better ways to make steel. In the 1890s, Carnegie's people created a new method. It was called the open-hearth process. Now the company could manufacture steel even faster.

Many of the company's workers were immigrants. So was Andrew Carnegie. He felt close to them. He tried to treat them fairly. He gave them bonuses.

Carnegie said he supported the rights of unions. Unions are groups formed by workers to protect their rights and safety. Unions caused a lot of tension in the company. Sometimes workers didn't think they were being treated fairly. They went on strike. They refused to work until their demands were met. During a strike in 1892, company managers hired men who were not in a union. They shot and killed several workers. Carnegie was mortified.

A man named Charles Schwab made peace with the workers. He became president of the Carnegie Steel Company. Schwab wanted to reorganize the company. He wanted to make it more efficient. It would make more money.

Charles M. Schwab (*center*) was president of the U.S. Steel Corporation. Schwab risked his company to produce an "H" beam that made it possible to build skyscrapers. He lost everything in the 1929 stock market crash and died broke in 1939.

Steel mills produced several products. Schwab wanted each factory to manufacture only one product. One factory could make girders. Another factory could make railroad ties. He suggested other ways to make the company bigger.

Carnegie sold the company in 1901 and retired. Schwab and J. P. Morgan bought it. They paid Carnegie

Carnegie Spends His Money

Andrew Carnegie was very rich when he retired. In twenty years, Carnegie gave away a lot of money. He gave money to the town in Scotland where he was born. He also gave money to the city of Pittsburgh where he lived. He wanted to help people.

Carnegie remembered how he loved to read when he was a boy. He had learned so much from books. He wanted everyone to read. So he built nearly 3,000 libraries in the United States and around the world.

J. P. Morgan (1837–1913) was an American banker who turned his family fortune into a huge empire through his dealings in the railroad and steel industries. He lent gold to the American government before the existence of a national bank, helping the country avoid major economic disaster. He was often criticized for his harsh, demanding way of doing business. He generously supported the arts.

$480 million. The company became part of the United States Steel Corporation. In retirement, Carnegie devoted his time to giving away money.

The United States Steel Corporation mined the raw iron ore. It owned factories where the iron ore was turned into steel. It even sold the final product. Because it controlled most of the steel industry, it was a monopoly.

It was big, powerful, and ruthless. It drove smaller companies out of business. The company grew so large that the government broke it up.

3
Black Gold

For centuries, oil bubbled from the ground in Pennsylvania. Sometimes oil covered the surfaces of creeks in the woods. Native Americans used oil for paint, medicine, and fuel.

White men saw the oil, too. But they didn't know what to do with it. Some of them bottled it. They sold it as fake medicine.

By the 1850s, George Bissell and Professor Benjamin Silliman Jr. realized oil could be used for lights, but it needed to be removed from the earth and refined. Kerosene comes from refined oil.

In 1858, the Pennsylvania Rock Oil Company searched for oil deposits in Pennsylvania. Bissell was a part owner. The company wanted to sell oil to light lamps. They thought oil would be cheaper to use than whale oil.

Whales were becoming endangered because too many had already been killed.

They searched for a year and almost gave up. But they finally struck oil in Titusville, Pennsylvania. The man in charge was Edwin L. Drake. He was a part-time train conductor.

Soon western Pennsylvania became famous for oil. Companies popped up all over. Oil rigs were everywhere. Oil became so valuable it was called black gold.

John D. Rockefeller was a bookkeeper. In 1870, he started a company with two partners. They called it the Standard Oil Company. Most people in the oil industry

Standard Oil of California, or "SoCal," is shown here in 1913. Called the Pacific Coast Oil Company in 1895 when it was founded, it was acquired by John D. Rockefeller's Standard Oil Trust in 1900. In 1911, when the trust was broken up, the company reformed as the Standard Oil Company of California. Since the twentieth century, the company, renamed Chevron, has been involved in a variety of environmental and human-rights problems.

were disorganized. Rockefeller was smart and very organized. The oil business was divided into three parts: production, refinement, and sales. Rockefeller wanted his company to control each part. Rockefeller wanted to own the land where oil could be found. He struck special deals with some of the oil producers. Some folks didn't think these deals were fair. The Standard Oil Company used sneaky tactics. These tactics drove many companies out of business. But Rockefeller became the richest man in the world.

When oil comes out of the ground, it is called crude. To be useful, it must be refined. Rockefeller opened an oil refinery in Cleveland, Ohio. He bought many of the other refineries.

Rockefeller also wanted to control how oil reached people. The Standard Oil Company made special deals with the railroads. It got cheaper rates than other companies because it shipped so much oil. It was illegal for the railroads to give Standard Oil discounts, so they did it in secret.

The Standard Oil Company's marketing department was one of the best in the world. They set up local shops where customers could go for service. That was a very good idea.

The Standard Oil Company was soon the biggest oil company in the country. It became the Standard Oil Trust in 1882.

Muckraking

Ida Tarbell was a writer. She wrote for *McClure's Magazine*. She said that the Standard Oil Company used shady methods. Many people read her articles. In 1904, the articles were published in a book. It was called *The History of the Standard Oil Company.*

Politicians read her work. They agreed that the companies behaved badly. They passed bills. They wanted to prevent the bad things from happening.

Ida Tarbell was the first "muckraker." She was also one of the first women journalists. She inspired many other people to write muckraking articles.

Muckrakers write about shifty things that companies do. People still muckrake today. A recent example is *Fast Food Nation* by Eric Schlosser. It is about fast-food companies selling unhealthy meals to people.

In 1892, the Ohio Supreme Court made an important decision. It decided that the Standard Oil Trust had to be broken up. It was too powerful. It controlled too much of the oil business.

The Standard Oil Trust tried to stay together. Its lawyers used tricks. It moved its offices from Cleveland to

Ida Tarbell (1857–1944), shown here in the late 1800s, finally wrote her autobiography when she was eighty years old. She was very modest about her accomplishments, although her book *The History of the Standard Oil Company* was, and still is, considered by some historians to be the most important business book ever written.

Using Less Oil

The United States is very dependent on oil. But the United States has almost run out of its own oil. Now, it must rely on oil from other countries. Much of this oil is located in the Middle East. For many years, the United States has been politically involved with countries there. This has made other countries angry. The United States has fought wars over oil.

Many people drive large cars that use a lot of gasoline. Their engines send poisons into the air. This is bad for the environment. It also makes people sick. Scientists are developing renewable energy sources like solar power and biofuel. These forms of energy will be much cheaper and safer to use.

New Jersey. The United States Supreme Court said it was not good enough. In 1911, the Court broke the Standard Oil Trust into lots of small companies. Many of these companies make up the bulk of the oil business today.

Glossary

Bessemer process (**Bess-EH-mur PRAH-sess**) A method for making steel. Invented by Henry Bessemer in 1855.

crude oil (**KROOD OYL**) Raw oil as it is pumped out of the ground.

deposits (**dih-PAH-zihtz**) Natural materials that have accumulated underground.

displaced (**dis-PLAYCED**) To be pushed away from one's home.

exploitation (**ek-sploy-TAY-shun**) Using a person or persons for selfish purposes.

immigrant (**IH-muh-grint**) Someone who leaves home to move to a new country.

magnate (**MAG-nate**) An extremely powerful businessman.

Mississippi River (**MISS-ih-sip-ee RIH-ver**) A body of water that flows from Minnesota to the Gulf of Mexico.

monopoly (**muh-NAH-puh-lee**) Businesses owned by one group, which can prevent competition.

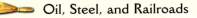

muckraker (**MUK-ray-kerr**)   A person who exposes the immoral and illegal conduct of well-known people or companies.

oil rig (**OYL rig**)   Machinery used for drilling an oil well.

public transportation (**PUH-blik tranz-por-TAY-shun**)   A bus, train, or other vehicle that is available to everyone.

refined oil (**re-FYND OYL**)   Oil that has its impurities filtered out of it so that it can be used.

renewable energy (**re-NEW-ah-bull EN-er-gee**)   Energy from the sun, wind, or water that can replace itself as it is used.

ruthless (**ROOTH-less**)   Having no feelings for the suffering of others.

strike (**STRYK**)   When people refuse to work as a way to protest unfair treatment by a company.

tram rail (**TRAM rayl**)   The track that streetcars run on.

trust (**TRUHST**)   A group of businesses that controls many different aspects of an industry.

union (**YOON-yun**)   A group of workers that have come together to fight for their rights.

Web Sites

Due to the changing nature of Internet links, the Rosen Publishing Group, Inc., has developed an online list of Web sites related to the subject of this book. This site is updated regularly. Please use this link to access the list:

http://www.rosenlinks.com/aistc/oisr

Primary Source Image List

Cover: Repairing railroad line, photograph by Andrew J. Russell, circa 1863, Virginia, Confederate States of America; Medford Historical Society/Corbis.

Page 5: Trevithick's engine, 1801, the first passenger-carrying road locomotive. It was operated for the first time in Camborne, Great Britain. Hulton Archive.

Page 6: "The First Steam Railroad Passenger Train in America," by Brown, cut-paper silhouette, 30 cm. by 47 cm., created in 1831. First published in Boston, 1870, by the Antique Publishing Company. Library of Congress.

Page 9: Map showing the Danville, Urbana, Bloomington & Pekin Railroad, 69 cm. by 64 cm., G. W. & C. B. Colton & Co., New York, 1869. Library of Congress, Geography and Map Division.

Page 11: Golden spike, 1869, housed in the Stanford University Museum of Art in Palo Alto, California.

Page 12: The only known authentic photograph of Casey Jones in the cab of an engine. This is a detail from the photo of Engine 638. Photograph by J. E. France, 1898. From the Bruce Gurner Collection, Water Valley Casey Jones Railroad Museum, Water Valley, MS.

Page 13: Title page from sheet music for voice and piano, *In the Baggage Coach Ahead* by Gussie L. Davis, published in 1896 by Howley, Haviland & Company, New York. From the Rare Book, Manuscript, and Special Collections Library, Duke University.

Page 15: Poor boys advertising art for W. Duke Sons & Company, Duke Cigarettes, lithography and printing by Knapp & Company, 1850–1920. Rare Book, Manuscript, and Special Collections Library, Duke University.

Page 16: From Henry Bessemer's *An Autobiography*. London: Offices of Engineering, 1905. First edition, published posthumously in London. University of Rochester.

Page 18: Charles M. Schwab standing with two unidentified men near train, 1919, photograph for the *Chicago Daily News*, black and white, glass, 5 in. by 7 in. *Chicago Daily News* negatives collection, Chicago Historical Society.

Page 20: Portrait of J. P. Morgan Bettmann/Corbis.

Page 22: General view, Standard Oil Company, Richmond, California. Photographic print, gelatin silver, 9 in. by 49.5 in., April 23, 1913, West Coast Art Company. Library of Congress, Prints and Photographs Division.

Page 25: Ida Tarbell, circa late 1880s. Underwood.

Index

About the Author

Jesse Jarnow is a Brooklyn-based writer and editor. He writes mostly about loud music and big explosions. His work has appeared in numerous magazines, including *Signal to Noise, Relix, 11211, Hear/Say*, and *The Anonymous Church of the Hypocritical Prophet*. He is a graduate of the Oberlin College creative writing department and a former member of the Studio 77 Art Collective.